Break a Leg

A Full-Length Play

By

JOHN O'BRIEN

THE DRAMATIC PUBLISHING COMPANY

*** NOTICE ***

Printed in the United States of America

(BREAK A LEG)

ISBN 0-87129-489-3

BREAK A LEG

A Full-Length Play

for Four Men, Twelve Women, Extras

CHARACTERS

Polly O'Connor, Les Peterson, Larry, Harry, Gertrude, Maggie, Molly, Annie, Judy, Susan, Jennifer
The Author
The Dancer
The Male Voice
The Sea Captain, The Bride and Groom
Romeo and Juliet
Portia (Merchant of Venice)
Shylock
Hamlet
Macbeth
Lady Macbeth
Seton
Doctor of Physic
Waiting/Gentlewoman
Portia (Julius Caesar)
Caesar
Brutus
Marc Antony
Calpurnia
The Three Witches
The Director
The Stage Manager
Dancers and Stagehands

TIME: The Present
PLACE: Tilton High School Stage

ACT ONE

SCENE: A high school stage.

AT RISE OF CURTAIN: There is pandemonium as a small army of Monsieur Hulots is trying to build a set that resembles a room. There are doors L and R, with French doors UC. To add to the bedlam, the ACTORS are performing voice exercises, yoga exercises, and meditation exercises. OTHERS are putting on makeup. POLLY enters down a side aisle and walks onto the stage.

POLLY (looking around the stage). All right, everybody, this is it. Lester? Lester? Lester? . . . Lester? . . . Lester? . . . Lester? . . . Oh, Les?

(LES enters.)

LES. You called?
POLLY. Seven times.
LES. I only heard you once.
POLLY. Your name isn't Lester?
LES. My name is Gregory.
POLLY. I know it's none of my business, but if your name is Gregory, why do they call you Les?
HARRY. Because he's good at arithmetic.
LARRY (as LES exits). Especially subtraction.
HARRY and LARRY. Yuk, yuk, yuk.

POLLY. Tell me he didn't say that. (HARRY turns and faces upstage. He raises an imaginary baton and the STAGEHANDS and ACTORS turn to face him.)

ALL. He didn't say that.

POLLY. Thank you.

LES. Any more questions?

POLLY. No more questions.

JUDY. I have a question.

POLLY. What is it?

JUDY. How did *you* know?

POLLY. How did I know what?

JUDY. My question.

POLLY. What question?

JUDY. What is it?

POLLY. What is what?

JUDY. This. (She holds up a strange object.)

POLLY. I don't know.

JUDY. Who does?

POLLY. Ask the stage manager.

JUDY. I did.

POLLY. What did she say?

JUDY. She said to ask the prop girl.

POLLY. What did she say?

JUDY. I'm the prop girl.

HARRY. Maybe it was left here from Junior Varieties.

LARRY. When in doubt, blame a junior.

HARRY. I blame my father.

LARRY. What for?

HARRY. He gave me his name.

LARRY. What's wrong with that?

HARRY. I'll be a junior all my life.

HARRY and LARRY. Yuk, yuk, yuk.

POLLY. Tell me he didn't say that. (HARRY turns upstage and raises the imaginary baton again. ALL turn toward him.)
ALL. He didn't say that.
POLLY. Thank you.
JUDY. I still don't know what it is.
HARRY. Whatever it is, it looks obscene.
JUDY. Everything looks obscene to you.
POLLY. Concentrate on *this* scene, will you, please?
GERTRUDE. Miss O'Connor?
HARRY (correcting GERTRUDE). *Ms.* O'Connor.
GERTRUDE. Ms. O'Connor?
HARRY. Don't you know nuttin?
POLLY. Just for tonight, you may call me Polly.
HARRY. My mother had a bird named Polly.
POLLY (to GERTRUDE). What did you want to tell me?
HARRY. She choked on a cracker.
GERTRUDE. Your mother?
POLLY. There's no hurry.
HARRY. My mother choked on the bird.
POLLY. The play isn't until tomorrow night.
GERTRUDE. I never know when to believe him.
POLLY. I never know when to believe *you*.
GERTRUDE. Why me?
POLLY. I thought you had something to tell me.
GERTRUDE. I did. I do.
POLLY. Well?
GERTRUDE. You may not like this, Polly.
POLLY. Try me, Gertrude.
GERTRUDE. How shall I say it?
POLLY. In the fewest possible words.
GERTRUDE (counting on her fingers). Five.
POLLY. Five what?
GERTRUDE. Words.

POLLY. Go ahead.
GERTRUDE. Six syllables.
POLLY. I believe you.
GERTRUDE. I have to leave early.
POLLY. Leave?
GERTRUDE. Early.
POLLY. Tell me she didn't say that.
HARRY. She did.
POLLY. How early?
GERTRUDE. Fifteen minutes.
LARRY. Nine hundred seconds.
GERTRUDE. Is it all right?
POLLY. Of course.
GERTRUDE. Don't you want to know why?
POLLY. No.
LES. I do.
POLLY. If she has to leave early, she has to leave early.
GERTRUDE. Exactly.
POLLY. It must be an emergency.
GERTRUDE. It is.
POLLY. You must have something you have to do.
GERTRUDE. I do.
POLLY. Some place you have to go.
GERTRUDE. I go. I mean, I do.
POLLY. Otherwise you would never ask to leave early tonight.
GERTRUDE. Tonight?
POLLY. Of all nights.
GERTRUDE. Not tonight.
POLLY. From a dress rehear . . . Did she say what I think she said?
HARRY. What do you think she said?
POLLY. Not tonight.
LARRY. That's what she said.

GERTRUDE. Tonight's no problem.
POLLY. No problem?
GERTRUDE. I can stay forever tonight.
POLLY. Gertrude?
GERTRUDE. Yes, Polly?
POLLY. I may call you Gertrude?
GERTRUDE. My mother does.
POLLY. That helps.
GERTRUDE. And when I'm at school, you're my mother.
POLLY. I am?
GERTRUDE. *In loco parenthesis*.
POLLY. I hope I'm worthy.
GERTRUDE. My father's a lawyer.
POLLY. I should have guessed.
GERTRUDE. Is it all right?
POLLY. If it's all right with your father.
GERTRUDE. I mean, what I asked you.
POLLY. You want to leave early?
GERTRUDE. I don't want to.
POLLY. I misunderstood.
GERTRUDE. I have to.
POLLY. But not tonight.
GERTRUDE. Tonight's no problem.
POLLY. Gertrude?
GERTRUDE. I can stay forever tonight.
POLLY. I hope you don't mind my asking.
GERTRUDE. I don't mind.
POLLY. That's very gracious of you.
GERTRUDE. My mother says I should be polite to everybody.
POLLY. She sounds like a nice lady.
GERTRUDE. She is.
POLLY. Gertrude, when do you want to leave early?
GERTRUDE. Two words. Four syllables.

POLLY. Get it over with.

GERTRUDE. Tomorrow night.

POLLY. Did she say –

HARRY (interrupting). Tomorrow night.

POLLY. I begin to grow aweary of the world.

LARRY. Somebody get her a chair.

LES (calling off). Props.

HARRY (hunching his back). A chair, a chair, my *kingdome* for a chair.

JUDY. Here's one.

LES. Not that one.

POLLY. Thank you.

LARRY. Look out. (POLLY sits and the chair collapses.)

HARRY. You gave her the breakaway chair.

JUDY. Sorry.

POLLY (getting up). Me, too.

HARRY. As King Arthur said when the impostor came to Camelot . . .

LARRY. It's not my knight.

HARRY and LARRY. Yuk, yuk, yuk.

JUDY. Can we mend it?

LARRY. Of course, we can mend it. It's a breakaway chair. It's meant to break.

GERTRUDE. I'll fix it.

POLLY. Gertrude?

GERTRUDE. Yes, Polly?

POLLY. Put . . . the . . . chair . . . down.

GERTRUDE. Yes, Polly.

POLLY. Come here.

GERTRUDE. I am here.

POLLY. Tell me something. And go slow, because I don't always understand the first time.

GERTRUDE. What do you want to know? My mother says we

should never keep secrets.

POLLY. She sounds like a nice lady.

GERTRUDE. She is.

POLLY. Seven words. Ten syllables.

GERTRUDE. Don't keep me in suspense.

POLLY. How can you leave early tomorrow night?

GERTRUDE. Through the back door.

POLLY. Of the set?

GERTRUDE. Of the school.

POLLY. The back door?

GERTRUDE. My cousin is picking me up.

POLLY. Of the school.

GERTRUDE. To go to the wedding.

POLLY. Your cousin is getting married?

GERTRUDE. Her roommate.

POLLY. Your cousin's roommate is getting married.

GERTRUDE. My cousin is the bridesmaid.

POLLY. For her roommate?

GERTRUDE. For her roommate's bride.

POLLY. Your cousin's roommate is a man?

GERTRUDE. It's a big room.

POLLY. That helps.

GERTRUDE. Is it all right?

POLLY. If it's all right with your cousin.

GERTRUDE. Then I can go?

POLLY. Go?

GERTRUDE. To the wedding.

POLLY. Polly?

GERTRUDE. I'm Gertrude. You're Polly.

POLLY. I'm sorry. I'm not thinking straight.

GERTRUDE. Don't feel bad.

POLLY. I'll try not to.

GERTRUDE. My mother says we should never feel bad about our mistakes.

POLLY. She must be a nice lady.

GERTRUDE. She is. Besides, everybody does that.

POLLY. Does what?

GERTRUDE. Forget who they are.

POLLY. They do?

GERTRUDE. I do it all the time. But not in real life.

POLLY. Real life?

GERTRUDE. Just in the play. In the second half of the first act, when my husband comes in, I keep thinking he's my brother.

POLLY. Try to remember.

GERTRUDE. But my brother doesn't come in until the first half of the second act. The trouble is, the boy who plays my husband looks like my brother, in real life, and the boy who plays my brother reminds me of a kid I knew at camp, in real life. My mother says –

POLLY (interrupting). Gertrude?

GERTRUDE. Was I talking too much?

POLLY. You can't leave early tomorrow night.

GERTRUDE. I have it all worked out.

HARRY. Wait until you hear it.

LARRY. It's really neat.

POLLY. Neat?

GERTRUDE. You know how I get killed in the first half of the third act?

POLLY. I do.

GERTRUDE. And I fall down dead over here?

POLLY. Yes.

GERTRUDE. In front of the couch?

POLLY. Yes.

GERTRUDE. Now all I have to do is, when I die, I hit the deck.

POLLY. The deck?

GERTRUDE. And roll in back of the couch.

POLLY. Roll?

GERTRUDE. Like a barrel.

POLLY. A barrel?

GERTRUDE. Watch. (She hits the deck and rolls like a barrel out of sight behind the couch, then stands.) What do you think?

POLLY. Amazing.

GERTRUDE. He taught me how.

LARRY. All by myself.

POLLY. I'm impressed.

GERTRUDE. Here's the best part.

POLLY. What could be better than that?

GERTRUDE. Before I get killed, even before the third act starts, actually, during the intermission –

LARRY (interrupting). Wait until you hear this.

POLLY. I'm waiting.

GERTRUDE. Guess who's already behind the couch?

POLLY. Your cousin.

GERTRUDE. How could my cousin be there?

POLLY. Just a guess.

GERTRUDE. She'll be out in the car.

POLLY. If it's not your cousin, who could it be?

GERTRUDE (to LARRY). You tell her.

POLLY. Somebody tell me.

LARRY. Maggie.

POLLY. Maggie?

GERTRUDE. My understudy.

POLLY. I know who Maggie is.

GERTRUDE. When Larry stabs me –

POLLY (interrupting). Harry.

GERTRUDE. There I go again.

LARRY. I'm Larry.

GERTRUDE. I know.

LARRY. He's Harry.

HARRY. Hi.

GERTRUDE. When he stabs me . . .

POLLY. Shoots you.

GERTRUDE. Whatever.

POLLY. He stabs you in the first act.

GERTRUDE. I roll behind the couch.

POLLY. Like a barrel.

GERTRUDE. Watch. (She dies again, rolls behind the couch, then stands.) He wants to be sure I'm dead.

POLLY. He's not the only one.

GERTRUDE. So he comes after me. (She falls behind the couch.)

HARRY. Like this. (He leaps over the couch and drags Gertrude's lifeless body out front. Instead of GERTRUDE, the body is MAGGIE who was hidden behind the couch. GERTRUDE stands up behind the couch again.)

GERTRUDE. And he drags my lifeless body out front.

POLLY. Amazing.

GERTRUDE. But guess what?

POLLY. I can't.

GERTRUDE. It's not me he drags out.

POLLY. It's Maggie.

GERTRUDE. Right.

POLLY. Dressed like you.

GERTRUDE. And she'll be all curled up in a ball, like a ball. (MAGGIE curls up in a ball.)

LARRY. I taught her that.

GERTRUDE. Do you say "in a ball" or "like a ball?"

POLLY. Whatever.

LARRY. All by myself.

GERTRUDE. What do you think?

POLLY. Ingenious.

GERTRUDE (to the OTHERS). I knew she'd like it.

POLLY. Gertie?

GERTRUDE. Am I in trouble?

POLLY. Why do you ask?

GERTRUDE. Whenever you call me Gertie, I'm in trouble.

POLLY. I know I'm getting old.

GERTRUDE. You're young.

LARRY. And beautiful.

HARRY. Hubba, hubba, hubba.

GERTRUDE. You're so out of date.

HARRY. I like old movies.

POLLY. And I know that, as a person ages, the blood supply to the brain slows down, so you'll have to bc patient with me when I ask you this. I don't mean to pry, but I'm curious. How . . . can . . . you . . . go . . . to . . . your . . . cousin's . . . wedding . . .

GERTRUDE. My cousin's roommate.

POLLY. I'm sorry.

GERTRUDE. That's all right.

POLLY. Do you forgive me?

GERTRUDE. There's nothing to forgive. My mother says –

POLLY (interrupting). Gert?

GERTRUDE. Now I *am* in trouble.

POLLY. How can you go to your cousin's wombmate's . . . (She corrects herself.) . . . *roommate's* wedding if you are lying behind a couch?

LARRY. Rolled up in a ball.

HARRY. Like a ball.

POLLY. In front of five hundred people, with a thousand eyeballs watching you.

HARRY. Nine hundred and ninety-nine.

POLLY. Did I miss something?

HARRY. My homeroom teacher is coming.
POLLY. So?
HARRY. He has a glass eye. I'm his favorite pupil.
LARRY and HARRY. Yuk, yuk, yuk.
POLLY. Somebody tell me he didn't say that. (HARRY turns and faces upstage. He raises the imaginary baton.)
ALL. He didn't say that.
POLLY. Thank you.
GERTRUDE. The secret is the French doors.
POLLY. What secret?
GERTRUDE. Instead of being shut, they'll be just a teenie bit open.
HARRY. They call it ajar.
GERTRUDE. Call what?
HARRY. When a door is a teenie bit open, they call it ajar.
GERTRUDE. Who does?
HARRY. Everybody.
GERTRUDE. I don't.
LARRY. When is a door not a door?
HARRY. When it's a jar.
LARRY and HARRY. Yuk, yuk, yuk.
POLLY. What about the French doors?
GERTRUDE. When Harry drags Maggie out front, I crawl out through the French doors.
POLLY. You crawl?
GERTRUDE. Like a snake.
POLLY. Didn't you forget something?
GERTRUDE. What?
POLLY. The audience.
GERTRUDE. They won't see me.
POLLY. How do you know?
GERTRUDE. They'll be watching Harry drag Maggie.
POLLY. You hope.

GERTRUDE. Magicians have a name for it.
POLLY. Hocus pocus?
GERTRUDE. Something else.
HARRY. Misdirection.
GERTRUDE. That's it.
POLLY. Are you a magician?
HARRY. Not me. My uncle.
POLLY. Your uncle is a magician?
HARRY. He was. He used to saw a woman in half.
LARRY. What happened?
HARRY. She retired.
LARRY. Where is she living now?
HARRY. San Francisco and Los Angeles.
LARRY and HARRY. Yuk, yuk, yuk.
POLLY. Tell me he didn't say that. (HARRY turns and faces upstage. He raises the imaginary baton.)
ALL. He didn't say that.
POLLY. Thank you.
GERTRUDE. Would you like to see it?
POLLY. It?
GERTRUDE. The whole thing.
POLLY. From start to finish?
GERTRUDE. We're ready when you are.
POLLY. I can't wait.
GERTRUDE. You should go out front.
POLLY. On the sidewalk?
GERTRUDE. In the audience.
POLLY. May I stand on the side?
GERTRUDE. Stand anywhere. Wherever you stand, you won't be able to see it.
HARRY. Wait a minute.
GERTRUDE. What's the matter?
HARRY. She doesn't count.

GERTRUDE. Why not?
HARRY. She knows the trick. She'll be watching for it.
POLLY. I promise to be misdirected. (She leaves the stage and walks to a side aisle.)
HARRY. Are you ready?
POLLY. I am ready.
HARRY. Roll 'em. (He brandishes a knife.)
GERTRUDE. Don't stab me.
HARRY. You killed my brother.
GERTRUDE. That's the first act.
HARRY. Nobody's perfect.
POLLY. You're telling me.
GERTRUDE. This is the third act.
HARRY. All right, all right. Where's the gun?
GERTRUDE (calling off). Props?
JUDY (exiting). I'll get it.
POLLY (calling off). No hurry.

(JUDY returns with the gun.)

JUDY. Here it is.
POLLY. We can stay forever tonight.
HARRY. Is it loaded? (The gun goes off in Judy's hand.)
POLLY. It's loaded.
JUDY. Sorry.
POLLY. Me, too.
HARRY. Ready when you are.
POLLY. Roll 'em.
GERTRUDE. Don't shoot me.
HARRY. You killed my brother.
GERTRUDE. Give me time.
HARRY. For what?
GERTRUDE. To pray.
HARRY. Make it short.

GERTRUDE. Dear God –

HARRY (interrupting). Long enough.

GERTRUDE. Don't shoot! (HARRY pulls the trigger but the gun fails to fire.)

HARRY. Bang. (GERTRUDE dies and rolls like a barrel in back of the couch.) You can't escape that easy. (To POLLY.) I put that line in.

POLLY. I noticed.

HARRY. Is it right?

POLLY. Is what right?

HARRY. Should it be *easy* or *easily*?

POLLY. Whatever.

HARRY. Here I come. (He leaps over the couch and drags Maggie out, curled up like a ball. GERTRUDE tries to escape unseen through the French doors which collapse on top of her. ALL freeze except POLLY who hurries back onto the stage.)

POLLY. Ger?

GERTRUDE. Can we do it again?

POLLY. Ger . . . grrrrrr.

GERTRUDE. Does that mean no?

POLLY. How would you like to be Maggie's understudy?

GERTRUDE. Maggie can't do it.

POLLY. Is she going to the wedding, too?

GERTRUDE. She has . . . laryngitis.

POLLY. Maggie, is that true? (MAGGIE nods affirmatively.) Let me see your throat. (MAGGIE stands and opens her mouth.) Say "ahh."

MAGGIE (loudly and clearly, as if auditioning for an opera). Ahhh.

GERTRUDE. I'll do it. I'll do it. I'll tell my cousin to tell her roommate to get married later.

POLLY. Thank you, Gertrude. That's very thoughtful of you. Are we ready?

HARRY (crossing DR). Ready on the right.

LARRY (crossing DL). Ready on the left.
MAGGIE (crossing DC). Fire.

(LES runs in with a fire extinguisher. He has on leather-soled shoes and, when he tries to stop, he slides across the stage.)

LES. Where is it? Where is it?
POLLY. No, Les. It was just a figure of speech.
LES. How was I to know?
POLLY. It's all right, Les.
LES. I was just doing my job.
POLLY. We'll call when we need you.
LES. At your service, sire. (He runs and slides off. There is a tremendous crash offstage.)
POLLY (calling off). Stage manager?

(ANNIE enters.)

ANNIE. Ready whenever you say, Cecil.
POLLY. You're not the stage manager.
ANNIE. I am now.
POLLY. Who appointed you?
ANNIE. She did.
POLLY. Where is she?
ANNIE. She's not here.
POLLY. I didn't ask you where she isn't. I asked you where she is.
ANNIE. Something personal came up.
POLLY. Personal?
ANNIE. In her private life.
POLLY. I see.
ANNIE. She has to rehearse.
POLLY. For a wedding.

ANNIE. How did you know?

POLLY. Just a hunch.

HARRY. Does the name Quasimodo ring a bell?

LARRY and HARRY. Yuk, yuk, yuk.

POLLY (ignoring LARRY and HARRY). She's not getting married?

ANNIE. She's a bridesmaid.

POLLY. A brides . . .

ANNIE. Maid.

POLLY. I'm sorry. I should have guessed.

ANNIE. That's the girl who carries the flowers.

POLLY. I know who the bridesmaid is.

ANNIE. She's the stage manager.

POLLY. Why don't *you* be the bridesmaid?

ANNIE. I know the play backwards.

POLLY. How about forwards?

ANNIE. Both ways.

POLLY. I know I shouldn't ask, but the stage manager isn't, by any chance, a bridesmaid at her roommate's wedding?

ANNIE. How did you know?

POLLY. Intuition.

ANNIE. You must have e.s.p.

POLLY. No, but I wish I had an a.s.p. to sit on.

ANNIE. Is that how you spell it?

POLLY (calling). Gertrude?

ANNIE. I'm Annie.

POLLY. I'm calling Gertrude.

ANNIE. You were looking at me.

POLLY. If I looked at a peach and asked for a pear, what would you bring me?

ANNIE. Two peaches.

POLLY. Gertrude?

GERTRUDE. Yes, Polly?

POLLY. Don't answer this if it's too personal.
GERTRUDE. That's all right.
POLLY. Is the stage manager your cousin?
GERTRUDE. How did you know?
POLLY. Just guessing.
ANNIE. They walk down the aisle together. It's so exciting.
POLLY. I get excited just hearing about it.
ANNIE. He gives her the ring. She gives him the finger.
POLLY. That sounds like a fair exchange.
ANNIE. She'll be all dressed in green.
POLLY. Green?
ANNIE. Sea green.
POLLY. I can't, but I am beginning to see red. (The stage lights turn red for two seconds.)
ANNIE. Just tell us when you're ready.
POLLY. When *I'm* ready?
ANNIE. I'll be right over there by the thing.
POLLY. The thing?
ANNIE. Against the wall.
POLLY. What thing?
ANNIE. The thing with all the switches on it.
POLLY. Oh, that thing. Some people call it the board.
ANNIE. Not me. I find life interesting.
POLLY. I'm glad somebody does. Are you ready?
ANNIE. Almost. (She exits L.)
POLLY (calling off L). No hurry.
ANNIE (from offstage). It's on the other side.

(ANNIE enters R.)

ANNIE. Is it on the left?
POLLY. Right. (ANNIE exits R. The auditorium is plunged into total darkness.) Thank you.

ANNIE (from offstage). You're welcome.

POLLY. Bring up the footlights, please. (Nothing happens.) Footlights, please.

ANNIE (from offstage). I can't find the switch.

POLLY. Why not?

ANNIE (from offstage). The lights are out.

POLLY. Does anyone have a match?

HARRY. I used to.

POLLY. What do you mean you used to?

HARRY. I quit smoking.

POLLY. Does anyone have a flashlight?

ANNIE (from offstage). I can't think of everything.

POLLY. Somebody think of something.

ANNIE (from offstage). What should we do?

POLLY. Grope.

HARRY. Oh, goodie.

POLLY. Never mind "oh, goodie," just find the switch.

GERTRUDE. I found it.

POLLY. Turn it on.

LARRY. Ouch.

POLLY. What's wrong now?

LARRY. That's not the switch.

GERTRUDE. What is it?

LARRY. Take a guess.

GERTRUDE. It's got two holes in it.

LARRY. It's my nose.

POLLY. Will somebody find the switch?

ALL (ad libbing). Ouch . . . my shin . . . my chin . . .

ANNIE (from offstage). I found it.

POLLY. Oh, goodie.

ANNIE (from offstage). What shall I do with it?

POLLY. Bring up the footlights.

ANNIE (from offstage). Just the foots?

POLLY. Just the foots. (The houselights come on.)

(ANNIE enters from R.)

ANNIE. Something's wrong.
POLLY. What did you say your name was?
ANNIE. Is.
POLLY. My mistake.
ANNIE. Annie. Short for Annabelle.
LARRY. You sure are.
LARRY and HARRY. Yuk, yuk, yuk.
POLLY. I forgot.
ANNIE. That's all right.
POLLY. You're a forgiving person.
ANNIE. I learned it from my father.
POLLY. He sounds like a nice man.
ANNIE. He is.
POLLY. Annie?
ANNIE. Yes, Polly?
POLLY. Why do you think something is wrong?
ANNIE. You wanted the footlights.
POLLY. Want.
ANNIE. These are the houselights.
POLLY. True.
ANNIE. Ergo, something is wrong.
POLLY. Ergo?
ANNIE. That means therefore.
POLLY. I see.
ANNIE. No. Therefore.
POLLY. Therefore.
ANNIE. I learned that in English.
POLLY. Did you?
ANNIE. Even though it's Latin.

POLLY. Is it?

ANNIE. We study logic in English.

POLLY. Do you?

ANNIE. Ergo is part of a silly jism.

POLLY. A what?

ANNIE. Silly jisms have three parts.

POLLY. Do they?

ANNIE. The last part starts with ergo.

POLLY. Live and learn.

ANNIE. That's a cliché.

POLLY. Is it?

ANNIE. My teacher says we should never use clichés.

POLLY. Just silly jisms.

ANNIE. Silly jisms help you to think.

POLLY. Can you think what went wrong with the lights?

ANNIE. You said the switch was on the right.

POLLY. It's on the left.

ANNIE. I said, "Is it on the left?" and you said, "Right."

POLLY. Annie, I apologize. You're right.

ANNIE. I have to be right. Stage managers can't afford mistakes.

POLLY. You're right. I mean, you're correct.

ANNIE. Especially the night before the show.

POLLY. You know when the show is?

ANNIE. How could I forget? It's the same night that –

POLLY (interrupting). The stage manager's cousin is getting married.

ANNIE. She's giving him her hand.

POLLY. How generous.

ANNIE. In matrimony.

POLLY. Never mind her hand. Just bring up the foots.

ANNIE. Just the foots?

POLLY. Just the foots.

ANNIE. Here come the foots. (HARRY and LARRY lie DLC

and DRC. They kick their feet in the air, then sit up.)

LARRY and HARRY. Yuk, yuk, yuk.

ANNIE. You're not funny.

POLLY. Just ignore them.

ANNIE. Footlights coming up. (The footlights come up.)

POLLY. Houselights out. (The houselights go out.) I'm going out front to see how it looks. (She walks off the stage to a side aisle and paces the side of the auditorium.) Stage lights on. (The stage lights come on.)

ANNIE. How is it?

POLLY. Fine.

ANNIE. What do I do next?

POLLY. Close the curtain.

ANNIE. All the way?

POLLY. All or nothing at all. (ANNIE crosses up and closes the curtain in the window of the set.)

ANNIE. That was easy.

POLLY. Wrong curtain.

ANNIE. Oh, you mean the shade. (She returns to the window and tugs at the shade, pulling it off its roller.) Did I do something wrong?

POLLY. I'm waiting for you to do something right.

ANNIE. Tell me by the numbers. I'm good in arithmetic, especially addition.

POLLY. One: walk toward me. (ANNIE walks toward POLLY.) Two: stop. (ANNIE stops.) Three: turn right. (ANNIE turns R and keeps revolving.) Stop!

ANNIE (after stopping). Is that four?

POLLY. Whatever. Walk offstage.

ANNIE. Is that five?

POLLY. Yes. (ANNIE exits L. There is a tremendous crash offstage.) What was that?

ANNIE (from offstage). I stepped in it.

POLLY. Will you step out of it, please?

(ANNIE enters with her foot wedged into a wastebasket.)

ANNIE. My shoe is stuck.

POLLY. Step out of your shoe. (ANNIE steps out of the shoe that is not in the basket.) The other one!

ANNIE (stepping out of the wastebasket). My toes are cold.

HARRY. If you think this is chilly, you've never seen Brazil.

LARRY and HARRY. Yuk, yuk, yuk.

POLLY. Face to the left.

ANNIE. Your left or my left?

POLLY. Mine. Yours.

ANNIE. You're getting me confused.

POLLY. Just walk off the stage.

ANNIE. Is that six?

POLLY. Yes. (ANNIE starts to exit L.) Take it with you.

ANNIE (turning back to POLLY). Take what?

POLLY. The wastebasket. (ANNIE walks back to the wastebasket and puts her foot back into it.) Carry it off. (ANNIE extricates her foot again and picks up the wastebasket, then exits. To ANNIE offstage.) Do you see the rope?

(ANNIE enters L.)

ANNIE. I see it.

POLLY. Pull it.

ANNIE. Hard or easy?

POLLY. Don't ask questions. Just pull the rope. (ANNIE exits L. After a moment, a drop curtain depicting a forest scene is lowered into the middle of the set.)

(ANNIE enters L.)

ANNIE. That's pretty.
POLLY. Annie?
ANNIE. My grandmother lives in a place like that.
POLLY. Annabelle?
ANNIE. That's what my mother calls me.
POLLY. Where is the wedding?
ANNIE. In the second act.
POLLY. The stage manager's cousin's roommate's wedding.
ANNIE. In a house.
POLLY. What house?
ANNIE. Boat.
POLLY. Make up your mind.
ANNIE. It's in a houseboat, on a houseboat.
POLLY. They're getting married on a houseboat?
ANNIE. The captain has a license.
POLLY. A license for what?
ANNIE. To marry you.
POLLY. He's not marrying me.
ANNIE. She.
POLLY. The captain is a she?
ANNIE. The first mate is a man.
POLLY. The first mate?
GERTRUDE. Polly?
ANNIE. Of the houseboat.
POLLY (to GERTRUDE). What?
ANNIE. Captain Ahab had a first mate.
GERTRUDE (to LARRY). You tell her.
POLLY. Tell me what?
ANNIE. And a second mate.
LARRY. It's tomorrow night.
POLLY. What is?
ANNIE. I wonder if he had a license.
LARRY. The play.

POLLY. What play?

ANNIE. He must have if he was a captain.

LARRY. *Teenage Terror.*

POLLY. Oh, that play.

GERTRUDE. Can we get started?

POLLY. That's a switch.

ANNIE. Which one?

POLLY (to GERTRUDE). Are you in a hurry?

GERTRUDE. A little bit.

POLLY. How little?

GERTRUDE. If I'm not home by –

POLLY (interrupting). I thought you could stay forever tonight.

ANNIE. She was speaking figuratively.

POLLY. Oh?

ANNIE. Forever was just a figure of speech.

POLLY. I see.

ANNIE. My English teacher loves figures of speech.

POLLY. Does she?

ANNIE. He.

HARRY. As I always say . . .

LARRY. What do you always say?

HARRY. With a figure like that, how come we never metaphor?

LARRY and HARRY. Yuk, yuk, yuk.

POLLY. Will you yuk, yuk, yuk over to the ropes and get rid of the trees, please?

HARRY. I'll do it. (He runs L to R.)

LARRY. Let me. (He runs R to L.)

(LES enters.)

LES. At your service, sire. (He runs and then slides across the stage into the wings. There is a tremendous crash offstage.)

POLLY. I'm going to count to three: one . . . two . . . (The drop curtain rises.) Thank you. (A drop curtain depicting a street scene lowers into the middle of the set.)

ANNIE. My uncle lives in a place like that.

POLLY. My mother was a nice lady. She brought me up to be polite. She said I should never scream. So I am going to whisper . . . (She speaks in a stage whisper.) . . . Get that thing out of here.

HARRY. I'll do it. (He runs R to L.)

LARRY. I got there first. (He runs L to R.)

(LES enters.)

LES. I know the ropes. (He runs and then slides across the stage into the wings. There is a tremendous crash offstage.)

POLLY (screaming). Get it out. (Drop curtains of every description go up and down in the middle of the set. Traveller curtains start moving L to R, R to L, and back again. Everything that can move does so. After a few moments, the chaos subsides and the set clears.)

ANNIE. Are you ready?

POLLY. Ready? Why should I be ready?

ANNIE. Do you want the curtain closed?

POLLY. What curtain? (ANNIE points to the proscenium curtain.)

ANNIE. This one.

POLLY. Is that a curtain?

ANNIE. It looks like a curtain.

POLLY. Close it. (ANNIE closes the curtain.) Thank you, Annie.

ANNIE. Any time.

(MOLLY comes from the back of the auditorium and stands in the aisle.)

MOLLY. Sorry I'm late. Are you ready?
POLLY. Ready?
MOLLY. For me.
POLLY (pretending not to know MOLLY). You?
MOLLY. I'm Molly, Polly.
POLLY. Molly Polly?
MOLLY. I'm Molly. You're Polly.
POLLY. Are you in the play?
MOLLY. I'm the mistress.
HARRY. Of who?
POLLY. Of what?
MOLLY. Ceremonies.
POLLY. Oh, *that* Molly.
MOLLY. That's me.
POLLY. I've missed you.
MOLLY. I've missed you, too.
POLLY. You also missed rehearsals for a week.
MOLLY. I've been tied up.
POLLY. How dreadful!
MOLLY. I have a new job after school.
POLLY. Congratulations.
MOLLY. I've been tied up learning the ropes.
POLLY. That makes sense.
MOLLY. Are you ready for me now?
POLLY. Ready? For you?
MOLLY. To do my thing.
POLLY. Your thing?
MOLLY. My speech.
POLLY. Ready when you are.
MOLLY. I'm ready now.
POLLY. It's your move.

MOLLY. Which side should I go up?
POLLY. Either side.
MOLLY. I hate decisions.
POLLY. No hurry.
MOLLY. Is it all right if I flip a coin?
POLLY. Why not?
MOLLY. Does anyone have a coin?
POLLY. I'm broke.
MOLLY (calling off). Prop girl! Judy? Is Judy still the prop girl?
POLLY. She was.

(JUDY runs on with a clipboard.)

JUDY. You called?
POLLY. *She* called.
MOLLY. A coin. Do you have a coin?
JUDY. It's not on the list of props.
MOLLY. Do you have one?
JUDY. I have a pocketful.
MOLLY. May I use one?
JUDY. Will I get it back?
MOLLY. *You* flip it. Heads, I go right. Tails, I go left. (JUDY flips the coin.) Which is it?
JUDY. That thing.
POLLY. What thing?
JUDY. The big bird.
POLLY. It's an eagle.
JUDY. Is that heads or tails?
POLLY. Tails.
JUDY. I only see the wings.
MOLLY. Which way did I say for tails?
POLLY. Left.

MOLLY. Your left or my left?

POLLY. It doesn't matter.

MOLLY. I have a terrible memory.

POLLY. Don't be so hard on yourself. (MOLLY goes up onto the stage and steps behind the curtain. From upstage, she tries frantically to find the middle opening. HARRY walks downstage of the curtain, from DR to DC, and opens the curtain. MOLLY steps out.)

MOLLY. I didn't ask for your help.

HARRY. I didn't ask to be born, but here I am.

POLLY. Are you ready?

MOLLY. Could I ask a favor?

POLLY. Why not?

MOLLY. Is it okay if I read it?

POLLY. You knew it last week.

MOLLY. I wasn't nervous last week. I wrote it on my sleeve.

POLLY. Ingenious.

MOLLY. Do you think the audience will notice?

POLLY. Of course they'll notice.

MOLLY. Will they mind?

POLLY. If you don't why should they?

MOLLY. I don't mind.

POLLY. I'm not surprised.

MOLLY. Are you ready?

POLLY. I hope so. I really hope so.

MOLLY. Should I go off and come on again?

POLLY. No.

MOLLY (clearing her throat). Do you have any water?

POLLY. Do it dry.

MOLLY (shouting). Ladies and gentlemen . . . Can you hear me?

POLLY. Yes.

MOLLY. If you can't hear me, let me know.

POLLY. I will.

MOLLY. My mother says I talk too soft. (She speaks slowly.) Ladies and gentlemen, tonight is the annual senior class play. Each year at this time, the seniors of Tilton High School put on a play . . . Am I going too fast?

POLLY. No.

MOLLY. My father says I talk too fast.

POLLY. What does your uncle say?

MOLLY. I can't hear you.

POLLY. Skip it.

MOLLY. Skip it?

POLLY. Skip it.

MOLLY (skipping as she speaks). Ladies and gentlemen –

POLLY (interrupting). Freeze.

MOLLY. Freeze?

POLLY. Freeze.

MOLLY (shivering as she speaks). Ladies and gentlemen –

POLLY (interrupting). Stand still.

MOLLY. Still?

POLLY. Still.

MOLLY (standing catatonically as she speaks). Ladies and gentlemen –

POLLY (interrupting). Relax.

MOLLY. Relax?

POLLY. Relax.

MOLLY (drooping like a rag doll as she speaks). Ladies and gentlemen –

POLLY (interrupting). Do it the way you did it before.

MOLLY. Before what?

POLLY. Do it the way you did it the first time you did it.

MOLLY. Last week?

POLLY. Tonight.

MOLLY. Ladies and gentlemen . . . Then I stopped to ask you if you could hear me.

POLLY. Don't stop.
MOLLY. That's the way I did it the first time.
POLLY. That's true.
MOLLY. So what should I do?
POLLY. Skip the interruptions.
MOLLY. Skip them?
POLLY. No. Don't skip them. Omit them.
MOLLY. Don't do them?
POLLY. Right.
MOLLY. Are you ready?
POLLY. I think so.
MOLLY. Let me know when you're sure.
POLLY. I'm sure.
MOLLY. Ladies and gentlemen . . . Why do we always say that?
POLLY. What?
MOLLY. Why do we always say that?
POLLY. Say what?
MOLLY. Ladies and gentlemen.
POLLY. I don't know.
MOLLY. It sounds old-fashioned.
POLLY. Then change it.
MOLLY. Gentlemen and ladies . . . Is that better?
POLLY. Much.
MOLLY. It still sounds old-fashioned . . . Men and women . . . Women and men . . . Is that better?
POLLY. Much.
MOLLY. I'll have to change it on my sleeve. Does anyone have a pencil? (She calls off.) Props?

(JUDY runs in with a pencil behind her ear.)

JUDY. You called?

MOLLY. Do you have a pencil?

JUDY (checking her list). It's not on my list.

MOLLY (pointing to Judy's head). What's that?

JUDY. My ear.

MOLLY. Behind your ear.

JUDY. That's *my* pencil!

MOLLY. May I use it?

JUDY. It's not a prop.

MOLLY. May I use it? (JUDY hands the pencil to MOLLY.) Thank you.

JUDY (to POLLY). Should I write pencil on my list?

POLLY. Please do.

MOLLY. I'm ready.

JUDY. May I have my pencil back?

MOLLY (handing the pencil back to JUDY). Stay close. I may have to make more changes. Females and males, tonight is the annual senior class play. Each year at this time . . . Isn't that something?

POLLY. Something?

MOLLY. Something wrong, in English, saying *annual* and *each year*?

(ANNIE peers through the curtain.)

ANNIE. Redundant.

POLLY. Thank you, Annie.

ANNIE. Any time. (She ducks back in.)

MOLLY. Should I change it?

POLLY. No.

MOLLY. Keep it redundant?

POLLY. Yes.

MOLLY. She has a pencil.

POLLY. I know she has a pencil.

MOLLY. You're the boss.

POLLY. Do it all the way through.

MOLLY. From beginning to end?

POLLY. Do you know it backwards?

MOLLY. I don't even know it forwards.

POLLY. Just read it.

MOLLY. Females and males, tonight is the annual senior class play. Each year at this time, the seniors of Tilton High School put on a play. Tonight is no exception.

(ANNIE peers through the curtain.)

ANNIE. Cliché.

POLLY. Thank you, Annie.

ANNIE. Any time. (She ducks back in.)

MOLLY. The play tonight is *Teenage Error*.

POLLY. *Terror*.

MOLLY. My mistake.

POLLY. We all make them.

MOLLY. It stars Larry Spencer as the Rifle Team captain, Rick O'Shay, and Susan Baldwin as the cheerleader, Meg O'Phone . . . I forget who wrote it.

POLLY. So do I.

MOLLY. The students, under the capable direction of Ms. Polly O'Connor, have worked long and hard to make this production successful. We sincerely hope you enjoy it. Thank you. (She curtsies. POLLY applauds. MOLLY tries in vain to find the curtain opening.) Where's the hole?

POLLY. Just get off. (MOLLY prepares to jump over the footlights into the orchestra pit.) Not that way!

MOLLY. Which way?

POLLY. Either way. (MOLLY starts off L, changes her mind, then starts off R.) What are you doing?

MOLLY. It's not my fault. I'm upset.
POLLY. *You're* upset?
MOLLY. It's been coming on for a long time.
POLLY. What has?
MOLLY. My boyfriend left me.
POLLY. I'm sorry to hear that.
MOLLY. For someone else.
POLLY. Maybe you'll get him back.
MOLLY. I can't.
POLLY. Why not?
MOLLY. They're getting married.
POLLY. Married?
MOLLY. Tomorrow night.
POLLY. Tomorrow?
MOLLY. Night!
POLLY. Where is the wedding?
MOLLY. On a houseboat.
POLLY. Did she say what I think she said?
HARRY. What do you think she said?
POLLY. A houseboat.
LARRY. That's what she said.
POLLY. Your boyfriend –
MOLLY (interrupting). My ex-boyfriend.
POLLY. Is the roommate of . . .
MOLLY. The stage manager's cousin.
POLLY. Small world.
MOLLY. It's not fair.
POLLY. You're telling me.
MOLLY. But I'll see it through.
POLLY. The boat?
MOLLY. My speech.
POLLY. Bravo!
MOLLY. The show must go on!

POLLY. That's the spirit.

MOLLY. Should I do it again?

POLLY. No.

MOLLY. Do I take a curtain call?

POLLY. You?

MOLLY. After the play?

POLLY. No.

MOLLY. I didn't think so.

POLLY. Just the actors.

MOLLY. And the actresses?

POLLY. Yes.

MOLLY. My father said I should get a curtain call, too.

POLLY. Did he?

MOLLY. He says, if I stay with it, by the time I'm twenty-one, I'll be at the pinochle of my profession.

POLLY. I believe it.

MOLLY. He wants to give me flowers.

POLLY. Does he?

MOLLY. A corsage.

POLLY. He sounds like a nice man.

MOLLY. I told him to give me the flowers before the play.

POLLY. Good thinking.

MOLLY. After my speech – before I go off – when I'm still up on the stage – where everyone can see me.

POLLY. Fine.

MOLLY. Should he come down the right aisle or the left aisle?

POLLY. It doesn't matter.

MOLLY. It does to him. He gets nervous if he doesn't know in advance.

POLLY. Nervous?

MOLLY. It runs in the family.

POLLY. The left aisle is fine.

MOLLY. Your left or my left?

POLLY. Mine.

MOLLY. His ticket is for the right aisle, in the first row, on the end. He always sits there. He was in the air force. He likes to watch the actors waiting in the wings.

POLLY. It's all right if he sits on the right.

MOLLY. If that's the right, why is this stage left?

POLLY. Thank you, Molly.

MOLLY. For what?

POLLY. For coming.

MOLLY. What time tomorrow night?

POLLY. Curtain at eight.

MOLLY. When should I be here?

POLLY. Seven thirty.

MOLLY. That's kinda early.

POLLY. Early?

MOLLY. I'm not sure I can make it that early.

POLLY. Come when you can.

MOLLY. From six to seven, I twirl.

POLLY. You twirl?

MOLLY. The baton. My mother says I have to keep it up. My father says it's all right to keep it up, but it has to come down sometime. My father is funny.

POLLY. He sounds it.

MOLLY. He reminds me of you. He sees the bright side of everything. I think I'll go now.

POLLY. Don't do anything rash.

MOLLY. Not me. I use skin cream. Good night, Folly. (She exits up a side aisle, whistling happily.)

POLLY. Somebody tell me she's gone.

HARRY. She's gone.

POLLY. Everybody on stage.

(ALL come out from behind the curtain.)

POLLY. All right, Everybody. Take five.

ANNIE. Five what?

POLLY. Minutes.

HARRY. Three hundred seconds.

GERTRUDE. Where should we take them?

POLLY. Take them . . . take them . . . just go away.

LES. How far?

POLLY. Behind the curtain. (ALL huddle against the downstage side of the curtain at R.) Get out of here, where I don't have to look at you. (ALL scurry behind the curtain. POLLY slumps DL against the side wall.)

(JUDY enters DR in front of the curtain and crosses to POLLY.)

JUDY. Polly?

POLLY. Do I know you?

JUDY. We're sorry.

POLLY. Me, too.

JUDY. It'll be all right.

POLLY. You think so?

JUDY. You know what they say about a bad dress rehearsal?

POLLY. What do they say?

JUDY. You know.

POLLY. Tell me.

JUDY. Bad dress rehearsal, good performance.

POLLY. Who says that?

JUDY. Everybody.

POLLY. Who is everybody?

JUDY. My aunt.

POLLY. How does she know?

JUDY. She was in show business.

POLLY. Was she an actress?

JUDY. She was a contortionist. She used to wrap her leg around her head.

POLLY. Do you think she could teach it to me?

JUDY. She can't do it anymore.

POLLY. I never could.

JUDY. Me neither.

POLLY. I can't do anything.

JUDY. That's not true. You're a great director.

POLLY. I am?

JUDY. And all the kids love you.

POLLY. They do?

JUDY. And we want you to know, we're ready when you are.

POLLY. Where have I heard that before?

JUDY. Just say the magic word?

POLLY. Which one?

JUDY. Roll 'em.

POLLY. That's all I have to say?

JUDY. That's all. (POLLY rouses herself for one last try.)

POLLY. Curtain. (The curtain opens. She walks out into the auditorium and speaks from the back.) Roll 'em.

(HARRY rolls from R and LARRY from L, their heads downstage. They meet DC and stand.)

LARRY and HARRY. Yuk, yuk, yuk. (A pistol shot rings out from the back of the auditorium.)

ALL (ad libbing). Polly? Polly? Ms. O'Connor? We didn't mean it. We're sorry. Polly? (Armed with flashlights, ALL run up the aisles and out of the auditorium. The curtain closes and the houselights go up.)

ACT TWO

SCENE: The houselights go out. Lights come up on the front of the curtain. POLLY and JUDY are onstage DL, as in the ending of Act I.

JUDY. She used to wrap her leg around her head.
POLLY. Do you think she could teach it to me?
JUDY. She can't do it anymore.
POLLY. I never could.
JUDY. Me neither.
POLLY. I can't do anything.
JUDY. That's not true. You're a great director.
POLLY. I am?
JUDY. And all the kids love you.
POLLY. They do?
JUDY. And we want you to know, we're ready when you are.
POLLY. Where have I heard that before?
JUDY. Just say the magic word.
POLLY. Which one?
JUDY. Roll 'em.
POLLY. That's all I have to say?
JUDY. That's all. (POLLY rouses herself for one last try.)
POLLY. Curtain. (The curtain opens. She walks out into the

auditorium and speaks from the back.) Roll 'em.

(HARRY rolls from R and LARRY from L, their heads downstage. They meet DC and stand.)

LARRY and HARRY. Yuk, yuk, yuk. (A pistol shot rings out from the back of the auditorium.)

ALL (ad libbing). Polly? Polly? Ms. O'Connor? We didn't mean it. We're sorry. Polly? (ALL run off the stage and up the aisles.) Where is she? She's not here. She's over there. The shot came from over there. She's over here. I see her. That's not her. Yes, it is. No, it's not. Who is it? We'll never find her. (Wailing.) Polly? (Spotlights, used as searchlights, flash around the auditorium, finally intersecting on POLLY who stands at the side of the auditorium, holding a gun.) Polly?

POLLY. Yuk, yuk, yuk.

HARRY. We'll be good, won't we?

LARRY. Yes.

AMY. Yes.

GERTRUDE. Yes.

POLLY. No more clowning around? (A spot follows the CAST as they walk back onstage.)

LES. No.

JUDY. No.

MAGGIE. No.

POLLY. All right, one last chance.

HARRY. Yip.

LARRY. Pee.

POLLY. Curtain. (The curtain opens and the stage lights come up.)

ANNIE. Places. (The CAST scurries backstage. POLLY stands DL.)

(SUSAN steps from R and stands outside the R door of the set. She stares off into space.)

POLLY. Susan?

SUSAN. Yes?

POLLY. What are you doing?

SUSAN. I'm getting into character.

POLLY. Get into character tomorrow night. Tonight, just get into the room. And don't stop for anything. If anything goes wrong, keep going. Say something, anything. Ad lib. Improvise. But don't stop! (SUSAN opens the door and steps into the room.)

(Just as SUSAN turns to close the door behind her, the AUTHOR comes down the aisle.)

AUTHOR. Hold it right there! (SUSAN freezes.)

POLLY. Who are you?

AUTHOR. Nobody move a muscle.

POLLY. You have no right to interrupt a rehearsal.

AUTHOR. Rehearsal for what?

POLLY. The senior class play.

AUTHOR. What play?

POLLY. *Teenage Terror.*

AUTHOR. Written by?

POLLY. Somebody. (The AUTHOR walks up onto the stage.)

AUTHOR. Somebody named Angela DeGeorge?

POLLY. How do you know?

AUTHOR (histrionically). I am Angela DeGeorge.

HARRY. Is that your real name?

AUTHOR. It is my pen name.

LARRY. What if you write with a pencil?

AUTHOR. I was passing through this area, on various artistic endeavors, making personal appearances at various autograph parties, visiting my various fan clubs . . . (HARRY and LARRY, standing behind the AUTHOR, pretend to fan her.) . . . when I noticed an advertisement in the newspaper. The advertisement mentioned my play, but it did not mention me.

POLLY. I'll ask the mistress of ceremonies to mention you tomorrow night.

AUTHOR. I have instructed one of my various attorneys-at-law to be in attendance tomorrow evening, so be sure your mistress of ceremonies follows instructions.

POLLY. She follows instructions to the letter.

AUTHOR (turning to the CAST). Good luck, children. (HARRY raises his imaginary baton.)

ALL. Thank you, Miss Angela DeGeorge.

AUTHOR. They remembered. (She exits up a side aisle.)

POLLY. Tell yourself that didn't happen.

SUSAN. Should I go out and come in again?

POLLY. Why not? (SUSAN steps outside the door of the set and stares off into space.) Whenever you're ready. (SUSAN snaps out of her trance and opens the door. As she steps inside the room, and turns to shut the door behind her, we hear someone blowing into a microphone through the public address system. SUSAN freezes.)

MALE VOICE (offstage, pompously a la the "Great Gildersleeve"). I'm sorry to interrupt the work of the school at this time, but I have a public service announcement. There is a blue houseboat blocking the mouth of the Tilton River. If it is not moved immediately, it will be towed. The registration number is six, six, six, dash, six, six, six. (A long beat. ALL look incredulous.) That number was six, six, six, dash, six, six, six. (Another long beat.) Thank you.

POLLY. Thank you.

MALE VOICE (offstage, after more blowing into the microphone). I'm sorry to interrupt the work of the school at this time, but it has come to my attention that the previous announcement did not get through to all the rooms. If you are in a room that is not receiving these announcements, please notify the office at once.
POLLY. What office?
LARRY. The principal's office.
POLLY. That wasn't the principal.
HARRY. It was the night school principal.
LARRY. The night school always meets on Thursday night.
POLLY. Will somebody, anybody, go to the office and tell the night school principal to take his microphone and shhhhhhhhhhut it off?
LARRY. I'll go.
POLLY. Thank you.
LARRY. Can I have a note?
POLLY. A note?
LARRY. So he'll believe me.
POLLY. Believe you?
HARRY. I'll go. I won't need a note.
POLLY. Good.
HARRY. He knows me.
POLLY. That helps.
HARRY. He's my homeroom teacher.
POLLY (pointing to her eye). The one with the . . .
HARRY. That's him. (He exits.)
SUSAN. Should we wait until he gets back?
POLLY. No.
SUSAN. I'll go out and come in again.
POLLY. Oh, goodie!
SUSAN. To make it seem more real.
POLLY. It seems real enough. (SUSAN steps outside the R door

of the set. She stares off into space, comes out of her trance, steps back into the set, closes the door behind her and crosses to the L door of the set.)

(JENNIFER enters from L and stands outside the L door of the set. She stares off into space.)

SUSAN (speaking through the door). The coast is clear. (JENNIFER snaps out of her trance, opens the L door of the set, and enters the room.)

(Just as JENNIFER turns to shut the door behind her, the DANCER enters L and glides past JENNIFER into the room.)

DANCER (to JENNIFER and SUSAN). Who are you?
POLLY. Who are *you*?
DANCER. I'm looking for the belly dancing class.
POLLY. The belly . . .
DANCER. Dancing.
POLLY. This is not happening.
DANCER. Is this room A, three, ten?
POLLY. I am hallucinating.
DANCER. The nice man said the class meets in room A, three, ten.
POLLY. What nice man?
DANCER. In the office.
LARRY. She's in the night school. They always meet on Thursday night.
DANCER. Will somebody tell me where to go?
POLLY. Lead us not into temptation.
GERTRUDE. I'll take her there.
POLLY. Thank you.
DANCER. Gertrude.

GERTRUDE. Hello.
DANCER. I thought you were at a play.
POLLY. You know her?
GERTRUDE. All my life.
DANCER. This is a nice place you have here.
POLLY. Who is she?
DANCER. Is this Home Economics?
GERTRUDE. She's my mother.
HARRY. My brother got arrested for taking home economics.
LARRY and HARRY. Yuk, yuk, yuk.
DANCER. Why is that funny?
POLLY. It's not.
DANCER. It's no joke to get arrested.
POLLY. Good-bye.
DANCER. What's wrong with taking Home Economics?
POLLY. Come again next week.
DANCER. I work in a bakery. I take home a cupcake every night.
POLLY. Good luck.
DANCER. I never gamble.
GERTRUDE. Come, Mother.
DANCER. She seems like a nice lady.
GERTRUDE. She is.
DANCER (as GERTRUDE leads her away). I still don't understand why it's so funny to get arrested.
SUSAN. Should we go out and come in again?
POLLY. Please do. (SUSAN exits from the room via the door at R. JENNIFER leaves via the door at L. Outside the doors, they stare off into space. SUSAN comes out of her trance, opens the door R, and enters the room. JENNIFER is still in a trance outside the door L. Just as SUSAN turns to shut the door behind her, the MALE VOICE speaks.)
MALE VOICE (offstage). I'm sorry to interrupt the work of

the school at this time, but it has just been brought to my attention that tomorrow night, one night from tonight, there will be held in the auditorium the annual senior class play. May I take this opportunity personally to urge all of you – faculty and student body alike – to tell your relatives and friends about this production and I personally urge you, yourselves, personally, to support the work of our young people. When all is said and done, they represent our future. Today's youth are tomorrow's adults. Thank you.

POLLY. Thank you. (SUSAN exits via the door R, goes into her trance, comes out of it, enters the room, crosses to the door L, and speaks through the door.)

SUSAN. The coast is clear. (JENNIFER snaps out of her trance. She tries to open the stage door L, but it won't budge. SUSAN tries to open it from the inside, but to no avail. JENNIFER gives up and crosses upstage of the set, passing by the French door UC, to the stage door R. She enters and crosses to SUSAN. Still trying to open the stage door L, SUSAN doesn't notice JENNIFER.)

JENNIFER. Looking for me? (SUSAN is startled.)

POLLY. Jennifer?

JENNIFER. What?

POLLY. Are you chewing gum?

JENNIFER. It makes me less nervous.

(LES comes running in. He tries to stop, slides across the stage, and comes to a screeching halt.)

LES. You called?

POLLY. Are you less nervous?

LES. I'm Les Peterson.

POLLY. Better luck next time.

LES. At your service, sire. (He runs and slides off. There is a tremendous crash offstage.)

POLLY. Jennifer?
JENNIFER. What?
POLLY. This is a play rehearsal.
JENNIFER. I know.
POLLY. You are an actress.
JENNIFER. Thank you.
POLLY. Actresses don't chew gum.
JENNIFER. Why not?
POLLY. Would you wear mittens to a piano lesson?
JENNIFER. No.
POLLY. I didn't think so.
JENNIFER. I have woolen gloves.
POLLY. I'm sorry I brought it up.
JENNIFER. Should we proceed?
POLLY. Proceed.
JENNIFER. Looking for me?
SUSAN. You?
JENNIFER. Are we alone?
SUSAN. Alone?
JENNIFER. Here.
SUSAN. Where?
JENNIFER. In the room.
SUSAN. What room?
JENNIFER. This room.
SUSAN. Alone?
JENNIFER. We are alone, aren't we?
SUSAN. Completely.
JENNIFER. There's no one else for miles around?

(STAGEHANDS enter, walk back and forth past the French doors, then exit.)

SUSAN. I forgot my line.

(LES opens the French doors, holding a script.)

LES. No one. (He shuts the French doors and exits.)
SUSAN. No one.
JENNIFER. Safe at last.
SUSAN. Completely.
JENNIFER. He'll never find us here.
SUSAN. Who?
JENNIFER. Him.

(The sound of piano keys crashing as HARRY, dressed in a villain's cloak, with a villain's mustache, enters L. He stands outside the stage door L. JENNIFER and SUSAN don't see him. Suddenly, JENNIFER starts to laugh.)

JENNIFER (giggling). I'm sorry.
POLLY. We all are.
JENNIFER (giggling). I got the giggles.
POLLY. Nobody's perfect.
JENNIFER (giggling). Every time I say *him*, I get the giggles.
POLLY. When you're finished, let us know. (As Jennifer's giggling starts to subside, SUSAN starts to giggle.)

(HARRY enters. ALL, except LES and LARRY, follow him on. They laugh and roll on the floor. POLLY stands and stares. Gradually, they become aware of her and stop, one by one, until there is dead silence. POLLY walks DC, faces the CAST, and raises an imaginary baton.)

POLLY. When I count to three, everybody laugh – one . . . two . . . three! (She points her baton. Nobody moves. She goes to JENNIFER.) Jennifer, if you laugh once more, just once, there will be no senior class play tomorrow night at

Tilton High School. (She crosses DR.) Proceed.
JENNIFER. Safe at last. (HARRY exits L.)
SUSAN. Completely.
JENNIFER. There's no one else for miles around.

(STAGEHANDS enter and walk back and forth past the French doors, then exit.)

SUSAN. Not that *completely*.
JENNIFER. I forgot my line.

(LES opens the French doors, holding a script.)

LES. No one. (He shuts the French doors and exits.)
SUSAN. No one.
JENNIFER. Safe at last.
SUSAN. Completely.
JENNIFER. There's no one else for miles around.

(STAGEHANDS enter and walk back and forth past the French doors, then exit.)

POLLY. Will somebody look at a script?

(LES opens the French doors, holding a script.)

LES. The problem is . . .
JENNIFER (taking it as her line). The problem is . . .
POLLY. I know what the problem is. What's the line?
LES. He'll never find us here.
POLLY. Thank you. (LES shuts the French doors and exits.)
JENNIFER. He'll never find us here.
SUSAN. Who?

JENNIFER. Him. (The sound of piano keys crashing as HARRY, dressed in a villain's cloak, with a villain's mustache, enters L. He stands outside the stage door L. JENNIFER and SUSAN don't see him. JENNIFER fights back a temptation to laugh.)

SUSAN. Who was that? (HARRY knocks on the door.)

JENNIFER (trying not to laugh). I don't know.

SUSAN. Who could find us out here where there's no one else for miles around?

(STAGEHANDS enter and walk back and forth past the French doors, then exit.)

JENNIFER. Let's open the door and see.

SUSAN. I'm afraid.

JENNIFER. Scaredy cat. (She calls through the door.) Who is it?

HARRY. Western Union. Messenger boy.

JENNIFER. What do you want?

HARRY. I have a wire. (He takes a thin strip of copper wire from his pocket.)

JENNIFER. Who is it for?

HARRY. It's for you.

JENNIFER. Who am I?

HARRY. Don't you know?

JENNIFER. Of course I know.

HARRY. Who are you?

JENNIFER. Marylou.

HARRY. That's who it's for. (SUSAN lifts the hem of her skirt and points to her slip.)

JENNIFER. Slip it under the door.

HARRY. I can't.

JENNIFER. Why not?

HARRY. You have to sign for it.

JENNIFER. I'll sign it in here and slip it back out.

HARRY. Sorry.

JENNIFER. Why not?

HARRY. Why should I trust someone I've never seen?

SUSAN. He's right.

JENNIFER. How do I know you're really from Western Union?

HARRY. Who else would have a telegram?

SUSAN. I never thought of that.

JENNIFER (to SUSAN). Open the door.

SUSAN. You open it.

JENNIFER. We'll open it together. (She and SUSAN tug on the door from the inside. HARRY tugs on it from the outside. The door comes off its hinges. HARRY enters the room, holding the door in his hands.)

SUSAN. You're not a messenger boy.

HARRY. That's what you think.

SUSAN. Who are you?

HARRY. I am . . . him. (Offstage, someone hits the low keys of a piano.)

JENNIFER (fighting off the impulse to laugh). It's him, him, him.

HARRY (sneering). He, he, he.

SUSAN. I'm getting out of here.

HARRY. I bring my own message.

JENNIFER. Wait for me.

HARRY. And the message is . . .

SUSAN. Which way should we go?

HARRY. You can't escape.

JENNIFER. We can try.

HARRY (still holding the door). The doors are locked.

SUSAN. We'll go out the window.

HARRY (standing in front of the window). But I am blocking the window.

JENNIFER. He's right. There's no escape.

SUSAN. Maybe the phone will ring. (The phone rings. SUSAN answers it.) Hello? (She listens and hangs up.) Help is on the way.

(LARRY appears at L, outside the open doorway of the set.)

HARRY. Too late for help now. At long last, I have you in my clutches. (LARRY enters the room.)
LARRY. And I have *you* in mine. (HARRY chases SUSAN and JENNIFER. LARRY chases HARRY. LARRY tackles HARRY. They crash into a flat, which topples.)

(STAGEHANDS run out to save the set. LES slides on and into a second flat, knocking it down. Amid screams and utter confusion, the entire set, like a house of cards, collapses. ALL freeze in disbelief.)

GERTRUDE (breaking her freeze). You know something, Polly? I don't think we should have done this play. We should have done a comedy where we could all relax and have fun. I was going to say it earlier, and I know it's kinda late now, but . . . Polly?
ALL. Polly? (They break the freeze and walk slowly downstage to observe POLLY. As though in a ritual, they lift Polly's rigid form above their heads and carry her, in slow motion, from DL to DR where they are met by several STAGEHANDS, wheeling out a single bed. They lower POLLY onto the bed and cover her with a blanket.)
JUDY. She needs a good night's sleep.
LES. She's been working too hard.
LARRY. She'll feel better when she sees us tomorrow night.
SUSAN. All we need is an audience.
JENNIFER. I'm always at my best with an audience.
HARRY. We all are.

GERTRUDE. Shh. We should let her sleep. She needs a chance to unwind. (ALL tiptoe upstage, backing up.)

ALL (in a stage whisper). Unwind, unwind. (The curtain closes slowly, leaving POLLY alone in the bed DR. A spot covers her.)

MALE VOICE (offstage). I'm sorry to interrupt the work of the school at this time, but I have a public service announcement. There is a blue houseboat, registration number . . . (He begins to get seasick.) . . . zero, zero, zero, dash, zero, zero, zero, h, h, h, h, blocking the loading dock behind the school. If it is not moved at once, I'm going to get seasick. (POLLY sits up slowly. The lights turn blue.)

(POLLY looks L and sees a wedding procession enter DL, led by a SEA CAPTAIN. ALL sway, as though unused to the motion of waves. The BRIDE wears a sea-green dress.)

CAPTAIN. Do you take this woman?

GROOM (holding his eyeballs open). Eye, eye.

CAPTAIN. Do you take this man?

BRIDE (holding her eyeballs open). Eye, eye.

CAPTAIN. By the authority vested in me . . . (He holds his vest.)

(HARRY sticks his head through the opening in the curtain DC.)

HARRY. Are you the captain?

CAPTAIN. I am.

HARRY. Are you the first mate?

GROOM. No, she was married once before.

ALL. Yuk, yuk, yuk. (HARRY goes back inside the curtain. The OTHERS exit L, speaking in a stage whisper.) Unwind, unwind.

(The curtain opens slowly. The rubble has been cleared. JULIET is standing on a balcony. As she speaks, ROMEO enters.)

JULIET. Were he not Romeo called, so Romeo/ By any other name would smell . . ./ (ROMEO squirts deodorant under his armpits.) . . . As sweet as that which we call a rose./ What's in a name?/ (ROMEO shrugs.) O, be some other part belonging to a man./ (ROMEO frisks himself, searching frantically for some other part.) Nor face, nor arm, nor foot, it is not hand./ What's Montague?/ 'Tis but thy name that is my enemy.

ROMEO. Shall I speak at this?/ Or shall I hear more?

JULIET. Wherefore are thou Romeo?/ Romeo?/ Romeo?/ . . . Line my forgot I.

(LES runs on with a prompting book.)

LES. O. (He exits.)

JULIET. O. (ROMEO, JULIET and LES start to exit L, walking backwards.)

ROMEO, JULIET and LES (as they continue their exit). Unwind, unwind.

(As ROMEO, JULIET and LES exit L, PORTIA and SHYLOCK enter R. As PORTIA speaks, SHYLOCK shuffles a deck of playing cards.)

PORTIA. When mercy seasons justice/ It is enthroned in the King of Hearts./ (SHYLOCK cuts the cards to reveal a King of Hearts.) But mercy is above this septic sway./ It becomes the throned monarch better than his crown.

(PORTIA and SHYLOCK freeze as HAMLET enters from L.)

HAMLET. And thus the sickliness of Hughie's natives is thought over with the resolution of a pale cast./ Thus cowardice doth make us all conscientious./ From whose bourn no traveler returns. (He freezes.)

PORTIA. It blesseth her that gives and her that takes./ It is twice blessed/ Upon the place beneath./ It droppeth as the gentle rain from heaven./ The quality of mercy is . . ./ Line my forgot I.

(LES runs on with a prompting book.)

LES. No strain. (He exits.)

PORTIA. No strain. (PORTIA and SHYLOCK freeze.)

HAMLET (breaking his freeze). For in that sleep of death what dreams may come?/ There's the rub. (He rubs himself.)/ Whether 'tis nobler in the sufferer to mind/ That is the question./ Or not to be . . ./ Line my forgot I.

(LES runs on with a prompting book.)

LES. To be.

HAMLET. To be. (HAMLET, LES, PORTIA and SHYLOCK start to exit R, walking backwards.)

HAMLET, LES, PORTIA and SHYLOCK (as they exit R). Unwind, unwind.

(LADY MACBETH, carrying a candle, enters L with a DOCTOR OF PHYSIC and a WAITING/GENTLEWOMAN.)

WAITING/GENTLEWOMAN. I would not have such a bosom in my body for the dignity of the whole heart. (LADY MACBETH sighs.)

DOCTOR (looking at LADY MACBETH). What a thigh is there.

LADY MACBETH. Oh, oh, oh. All the hands of Arabia will not sweeten this little perfume. Here's the smell of blood still.
WAITING/GENTLEWOMAN. Heaven knows what she has known. I am sure of that. She has spoke what she should not.
DOCTOR. You have known what you should not. Go to. Go to.
WAITING/GENTLEWOMAN. Go to where?
LADY MACBETH. Will these hands ne'er be clean?/ The Thane of Wife had a fife. (She toots on her fife.)
DOCTOR. Do you mark that?
LADY MACBETH. Hell is murky./ Why, then, 'tis time to do't./ Out . . . / Line my forgot I.

(LES runs on, holding a small white dog with black spots.)

LES. Damned spot.
LADY MACBETH. Damned spot. Out. (LES runs off with the dog. LADY MACBETH, the DOCTOR, and the WAITING/GENTLEWOMAN start to exit R, walking backwards.)
LADY MACBETH, the DOCTOR, and the WAITING/GENTLEWOMAN (as they exit). Unwind, unwind.

(BRUTUS and PORTIA enter L.)

PORTIA. Here in the thigh./ Giving myself a voluntary wound. (She drives a sword into her thigh and blood spurts out.)/ I have made strong proof of my constancy. (BRUTUS exits L.)

(BRUTUS returns with a mop and mops up the blood.)

PORTIA. I grant I am a woman/ But withal a woman that Lord Brutus took to wife.
BRUTUS. As dear to me as are the sad drops that visit my ruddy heart/ You are my true and honorable wife.

PORTIA. Not his wife./ Portia is Brutus' . . ./ Line my forgot I.

(LES runs in with a prompting book.)

LES. Harlot. (PORTIA slaps Les' face.)
PORTIA. Harlot. (LES, BRUTUS and PORTIA start to exit L, walking backwards.)
LES, BRUTUS and PORTIA (as they exit). Unwind, unwind.

(Three WITCHES enter R with a cauldron which they set down on the stage. They form a semi-circle around it as they speak.)

FIRST WITCH. 'Round about the entrails go/ In the poisoned cauldron throw.
SECOND WITCH. Eye of newt and toe of frog . . . (She takes these items from a sack and drops them into the cauldron.) . . . wool of bat and tongue of dog . . .

(LES runs on with the dog. The SECOND WITCH goes to the dog, pulls out its "tongue," and throws it into the cauldron. LES runs off.)

THIRD WITCH. Scale of mummy . . .

(LES drags on a mummy case which he opens to reveal a MUMMY. The MUMMY hands a bathroom scale to the THIRD WITCH, who then throws the scale into the cauldron. LES exits, dragging the case.)

THIRD WITCH. Tooth of wolf . . . (She pulls out one of her own "teeth" and drops it into the cauldron.)

WITCHES ONE, TWO, THREE. Double trouble, toil and double./ Cauldron, burn, and fire, bubble./ (All three WITCHES pop bubble gum and start to exit R, walking backwards. As they exit.) Unwind, unwind.

(CAESAR and CALPURNIA enter L.)

CALPURNIA. Oh, Caesar/ A lioness hath whelped in the streets./ Recounts most horrid sights seen by the watch./ (CAESAR looks at his watch.) I never stood on ceremonies . . ./ Line my forgot I.

(LES runs on with a prompting book.)

LES. Forth. (CAESAR slaps Les' face.)

CAESAR. Caesar is never fourth. Caesar shall go first. (LES, CAESAR and CALPURNIA start to exit L, walking backwards.)

LES, CAESAR and CALPURNIA (as they exit). Unwind, unwind.

(MARC ANTONY enters R, surrounded by a CROWD.)

ANTONY. And Brutus is an honorable man./ Yet Brutus says he was ambitious./ Ambition should be made sterner that stuff./ Come I to speak in Caesar's funeral. (ANTONY and the CROWD freeze.)

(MACBETH and SETON enter L and stand on the side of the stage.)

MACBETH. Signifying nothing/ Full of sound and fury./ It is a tale told by an idiot. (He looks at SETON.)/ And then is heard no more./ That struts and frets his hour upon the stage./ A pool player./ Life's but a walking shadow./ Brief candle, out, out. (He and SETON freeze.)

ANTONY (breaking his freeze). Oft interred with bones is the good./ Lives after them the evil that men do./ I come to bury Caesar, not to raise him./ Your ears lend me, countrymen. (The CROWD holds up ears of corn, then they and ANTONY freeze.)

MACBETH (breaking his freeze). And yesterday, and yesterday, and yesterday./ There would have been word for such a time. (He freezes again.)

ANTONY. Romans . . . Line my forgot I.

(LES runs on with a prompting book.)

LES. Friends.

ANTONY. Friends. (He and the CROWD freeze.)

MACBETH (breaking his freeze). Hereafter she should have . . . Line my forgot I. (LES crosses to MACBETH with the book.)

LES. Died.

MACBETH. Died.

SETON (breaking his freeze). Is dead, my lord . . . Line my forgot I.

LES. The queen.

SETON. The queen. (LADY MACBETH screams offstage. POLLY is startled and jumps out of bed screaming. There is a blackout.)

(The real DIRECTOR comes down the aisle in the darkness.)

DIRECTOR. Bring up the lights. Lights please. (The stage lights come on. The DIRECTOR walks up onto the stage.) Cast on stage.

(ALL except the DANCER come onstage. The real STAGE MANAGER enters.)

STAGE MANAGER. Should I keep the curtain open?

DIRECTOR. Yes.

STAGE MANAGER. Are we rehearsing the curtain call?

DIRECTOR. Not tonight. We'll run through it tomorrow night before the house is open. Agnes? Where's Agnes? (The AUTHOR steps out from the CAST.)

AUTHOR. Here.

DIRECTOR. You were perfect. You had me believing you really wrote it.

MOLLY. How about me?

DIRECTOR. You were great, too. You were all great.

ANNIE. No notes?

DIRECTOR. I have a thousand notes, but it's late and you're all tired, so I'm going to send you home. Oh, Sharon?

GERTRUDE. Here.

DIRECTOR. You handled those night school interruptions like an old pro. They sounded like part of the play. Was that really your mother?

GERTRUDE. That's what my father says.

DIRECTOR. Rosemary?

POLLY. Here.

DIRECTOR. It was perfect right up to the end. Your final scream was too realistic. You sounded really upset.

POLLY. I am.

DIRECTOR. Is something wrong?

POLLY. It's my mother's boyfriend.

DIRECTOR. What about him?

POLLY. He just eloped with my boyfriend's mother.

LARRY, HARRY and POLLY. Yuk, yuk, yuk.

DIRECTOR. Tell me she didn't say that. (POLLY raises an imaginary baton.)

ALL. She didn't say that.

DIRECTOR. I don't know why, but I still love you all. (POLLY raises an imaginary baton.)

ALL. We love you, too.

DIRECTOR. I'll see you all tomorrow night. Break a leg, cast. (ALL pretend to break their legs. SOME hop about. OTHERS writhe on the floor.) Crazy kids. Go away. Get out of here. All of you. (To the audience.) You, too. Good night. (There is blowing in the microphone. ALL freeze.)

MALE VOICE (offstage). I'm sorry to interrupt the work of the school at this time, but there seems to be some confusion as to class assignments. Because of excessive popularity of certain courses, we are forced to make some adjustments in scheduling. Maritime Navigation will be held in the swimming pool; Cake Decorating is transferred to the Teachers' Lounge; and Belly Dancing has been moved to the Home Economics room.

(A line of BELLY DANCERS, led by the DANCER, dances onto the stage in belly dancing costumes.)

DANCER. This is it, folks. (To the DIRECTOR.) Would you like to learn to dance?

DIRECTOR. No, thank you.

DANCER. I've just been teaching that nice man in the office. (She reaches up to her veil and pulls out a small object.) Oh, goodie. I found a marble. Baby-blue. My favorite color. (She puts the marble in her navel and continues her dancing. The CAST begins to dance around the catatonic DIRECTOR.)

MALE VOICE (offstage, over the loudspeaker). I'm sorry to interrupt the work of the school at this time, but we have a minor emergency here in the main office. In the confusion of so many schedule changes, we have misplaced a rather important object. A reward is being offered to anyone who finds a missing glass eye. It belongs to my favorite pupil. Yuk, yuk,

yuk. (The dancing continues as the curtain closes, then immediately opens again. The CAST bows.)

(A REPRESENTATIVE of the organization sponsoring the production enters from the wings.)

REPRESENTATIVE. Thank you. Thank you. It's been a wonderful experience and we couldn't have done it without the person we've all come to love *(insert Mr. or Mrs. –, the name of the "really real" DIRECTOR).*

(The "really real" DIRECTOR comes up onto the stage. The REPRESENTATIVE gives the DIRECTOR a box that holds a breakable gift. The DIRECTOR fumbles with the box. LARRY steps forward.)

LARRY. I'll do it. (He "accidentally" hits the box and the gift shatters onto the floor. The CAST freezes in a tableau of mock shock. The curtain closes.)

PRODUCTION NOTES

SET: An interior set, representing a living room, with two doors plus French doors or a window upstage. One window must have a shade that can be ripped off when necessary. Two drop curtains should be used: one depicting a Forest Scene and one depicting a Street Scene. Other drop curtains and traveler curtains are needed for movement in Act I.

COSTUMES: Costuming may be as simple or elaborate as the director desires. A villain's cape and mustache are necessary, as well as belly dancing costumes. The Sea Captain may have an entire costume but, at the very least, he must have a vest. A sea-green dress is needed for the Bride. The Shakespearean characters (who may be the other actors who have speaking parts or the actors used as Stagehands) should at least wear partial costumes to designate the various roles they play.

PROPS: *Act I:* Breakaway Chair. Coin. Couch. Fire Extinguisher. Flashlights. Gun and Bullets. Knife. Pencil. Script. "Strange" Object. Wastebasket.

Act II: Bathroom Scales. Bed. "Blood." Blue Marble. Box with Breakable Gift. Bubble Gum. Can of Deodorant. Candle. Cauldron. Deck of Oversized Playing Cards. Ears of Corn. "Eye of Newt." Fife. Flashlights. Mop. Mummy and Case (may be an actor in large case or fake mummy in small case). Piano Chords (recorded or live). Prompting Book. Sacks. Strip of Wire. Stuffed Dog with Spots and Removable Tongue (live dog may be used on first entrance). Sword. Telephone and Bell. "Toe of Frog." "Tooth of Wolf."

DIRECTOR'S NOTES

DIRECTOR'S NOTES

DIRECTOR'S NOTES

DIRECTOR'S NOTES

DIRECTOR'S NOTES